FIRST
FUN
ATLAS

First published in 2005 by
Miles Kelly Publishing Ltd
Bardfield Centre
Great Bardfield
Essex CM7 4SL

2 4 6 8 10 9 7 5 3 1

This title is also available in hardback

British Library Cataloguing-in-Publication Data catalogue
record for this book is available from the British Library

ISBN 1-84236-613-0

Printed in China

Editor
Neil de Cort

Editorial Assistant
Nicola Sail

Designer
Venita Kidwai

Picture Researcher
Liberty Newton

Indexer
Jane Parker

Consultant
Clive Carpenter

Production Manager
Estela Boulton

www.mileskelly.net
info@mileskelly.net

FIRST FUN ATLAS

Andrew Langley

Miles Kelly
PUBLISHING

How to use the maps

Maps can look very puzzling. What are all those squiggly lines and strange colours and shapes? How can you fit a whole town or country onto one page?

You can read a map – just like you are reading this book now! Instead of letters and words, the map uses symbols and colour codes to give you information. Therefore to read a map you need to understand the symbols.

A feature on a map is much smaller than it is in real life. Maps show places at different sizes. So one centimetre on a map might represent one kilometre (that's 100,000 centimetres) on the ground.

Reading a book may open up whole new worlds – and so does reading a map. Just looking at the page of an atlas will help you to imagine jungles or mountains or deserts. You can work out journeys and measure how far it is from one place to another. Maps can even help you to discover why people's lives are so different.

▼ Physical map pages

Here you will find information about what the land in each continent looks like. Does it have mountains and rivers, deserts or rainforests? Can you tell if it is hot or cold? You will also discover amazing animals and wonderful natural places to visit.

Europe

Europe is the second smallest continent in the world – less than a quarter the size of Asia. Yet it is also the most crowded, with its population contained in 47 different countries.

Europe is able to support such a large number of people because it is lucky enough to have good farmland covering half of the continent. But there is less space for wildlife. The European brown bear is one of the few big animals to live in Europe.

There is a wide variety of birdlife, as well as smaller animals such as badgers, foxes, deer, hedgehogs, squirrels and wild boar.

▲ Copper butterflies can live almost anywhere. They are tiny, growing to only 36 millimetres across their wings.

▲ This fallow deer is guarding her fa The white spots on their coats help camouflage them amongst leaves wh they live. The fawn may stay with its mother for more than a year.

▲ A red fox's natural habitat is woodland, but many have adapted living in towns. They mainly hunt for food at night. They will eat al anything, from rabbits and earthworms to fish and apples.

Best of Europe

HOTTEST PLACE
Seville in Spain recorded a high of 50 degrees Celsius in August 188

LARGEST SEA
The Mediterranean Sea covers about 2,503,000 square kilometres.

LARGEST
Britain island coveri square

26

Two types of maps

In your atlas you will find two different kinds of map. They are called physical and political maps. Physical maps show natural features, such as mountains and rivers, seas, lakes and islands. They would be there even if there were no people around. Political maps show countries and states, which would not exist without people.

This physical map of Europe shows the rivers, mountains and seas.

This political map of Europe shows the countries in different colours.

▼ Political map pages

Here you will find information about the places in each continent and facts about each country. You will also learn about the people who live there and what their lives are like.

▼ Grid lines

Can you see the numbers that run across the top of each page and the letters that run down the right of the border? These are called grid lines. You can use them to locate places on the map. For example, look for Belarus on the political map – its grid reference is D11. Trace a line with your finger across from D and down from 11 and you will find Belarus. See if you can find the grid references for Finland.

Europe
People and places

Europeans have changed the world.
Despite its small size, Europe has produced writers, artists...

▶ The grebe is a water bird that dives underwater to catch food such as small fish, insects, snails and shrimps. It is the only bird that can dive whilst carrying its young.

◀ The European peregrine falcon is the fastest animal in the world. It can dive at speeds of over 280 kilometres per hour, that is 75 metres a second.

LARGEST MAMMAL
Brown bears can grow to a height of 1.2 metres.

SLOWEST BIRD
The Eurasian woodcock can only fly very slowly, travelling 2 metres a second.

◀ Greece is very popular with tourists. They visit the islands to enjoy the hot sunshine and visit the beautiful old buildings.

QUIZ
Find the European countries, hidden in these jumbled up names.
OLD SCANT   ANGRY ME
MARK END   RAIN BIT
SIR USA   CAR FEN

▲ France is the most visited country in the world. The Eiffel Tower is one of its main attractions.

1. ANDORRA Andorra-la-Vella
2. BOSNIA HERZEGOVINA Sarajevo
3. CROATIA Zagreb
4. CZECH REPUBLIC Prague
5. ICELAND Reykjavik (belongs to Russia)
6. LIECHTENSTEIN Vaduz
7. LUXEMBOURG Luxembourg
8. MACEDONIA Skopje
9. MALTA Valletta
10. MONACO Monaco
11. NETHERLANDS Amsterdam, The Hague
12. SAN MARINO San Marino
13. SLOVENIA Ljubljana
14. SWITZERLAND Bern
15. VATICAN CITY Vatican City

29

◀ Using a compass

A compass has a small needle in it that always points to the north (N). This helps you to find out where you are when studying a map. For example, it can help you to find which way you need to walk to get to a particular place .

Reading symbols on a map

Find out how to read the maps in this atlas by looking at the land colours and symbols used for the different features.

Desert   Grassland or forest   Mountains

POLAND UKRAINE
National borders

HIMALAYAS
Mountain range

■Warsaw
Capital city

River

SAHARA DESERT
Desert

Lake Superior
Lake

Earth in space

Imagine you are far out in space. You turn and look back at the planet we call Earth. What does it look like? It is round like a ball, and coloured, mostly blue and green with smudges of white.

It is also small — much smaller than most of the other planets that are near us. Some of these are huge, and could swallow up the Earth many times over. But, even bigger, is the Sun, a giant mass of fire and flame that is the brightest thing in our small corner of space. The Earth gets all its heat, light and energy from the Sun.

If you watched for long enough, you would see that the Earth does not stay in one place. It moves in a big circle around the Sun. This circle is called Earth's orbit. One whole journey around the Sun takes a year, or just over 365 days.

▲ The Moon

The Earth has a rocky ball, the Moon, that circles around it as it moves through space. It is one-quarter the size of the Earth. The Moon's surface is full of great holes called craters.

Pluto

Uranus

Saturn

Neptune

Jupiter

Mercury

Venus

Mars

Earth

▲ Spinning in space

Earth does not just move through space, it also spins round, like a top. Imagine a line drawn through the middle of the Earth from top to bottom. The Earth spins around that line, making a complete turn every 24 hours – a day and a night.

▼ Parts of the Earth

The Earth is split up into lots of layers, almost like an onion. If you could cut open the Earth you would be able to see all the different layers inside. The outside layer is called the crust. This is up to 50 kilometres deep in some places, but compared to the whole Earth it is very small. If the Earth was an apple, the crust would be as thick as its skin! The next layer is called the mantle. This is a layer of soft, hot rock that is nearly 2,900 kilometres thick. After this is the outer core which is made up mostly of molten metals, iron and nickel. In the middle is the inner core, where temperatures reach as high as 7,000 degrees Celsius.

▲ Poles and the Equator

At the very top of the world is the North Pole. At the bottom is the South Pole. And halfway between is an imaginary line called the Equator. The Equator is the part of the world nearest to the Sun, so it is always hot. The poles are furthest from the Sun, so they are cold.

▼ The seasons

The Earth tilts over slightly as it spins around. This means that for half of the year the top half of the Earth is tilted towards the Sun. This gives us the warmer seasons of spring and summer. When the Earth is tilted away from the Sun, we have the colder seasons of autumn and winter.

▶ Day and night

The Earth is constantly spinning like a top. At any time, the Sun only shines on one half of the Earth's surface. As the Earth spins around, the sunshine moves onto a different part of the surface. On the side of the Earth where the Sun is shining, it is light and day. On the side of the Earth that is facing away from the Sun, it is dark and night.

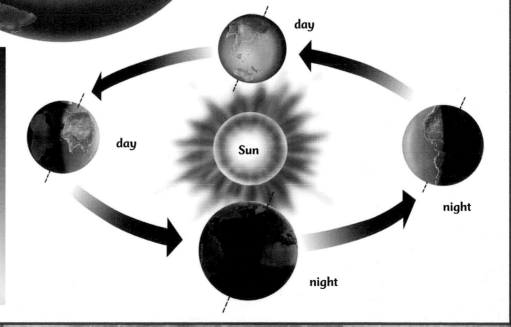

Looking at the Earth

How can we know what the Earth looks like? If you were an astronaut you could see it very well from your spacecraft. But the rest of us have to stay on the Earth's surface. We can't see the shape of a whole coastline or mountain or river. We can't tell how far it is across an ocean or between two cities.

Instead, we look at a map of the Earth. A map is a diagram, which shows where things are on the Earth's surface. Each kind of feature has its own sign or symbol. Symbols come in many different lines, colours and shapes to show rivers, mountains, towns, and so on.

There are many kinds of map. Some show the main features, using different colours for rainforest, desert or highland areas. Others use boundary lines and colours to show how the world is divided up into countries and states. Maps can be big or small. A map can show the whole world — or just your street!

▲ Continent map
This is the continent of Oceania. You can see Australia, New Zealand, and the small islands in the Pacific Ocean.

▶ Country map
Maps like this one of Australia show you where different towns and cities are. They will also tell you where to find other land features, such as mountains, rivers, lakes and deserts.

◀ Eye in the sky

Modern mapmakers use photographs taken from high in the sky by satellites or aircraft. Special machines transfer the shapes from the photos onto a sheet of paper. Mapmakers can also measure distances from these photographs. All this information is stored in a computer, which can then be used to control a drawing machine called a plotter.

▶ Round into flat

An exact map of the world would be a globe or sphere. But how do you draw this onto a flat piece of paper? One early method was to peel the Earth like an orange, then spread the peel out in sections (see the picture on the right). A better way was invented by Mercator in 1538. He wrapped a sheet of paper in a tube shape around a globe map, then copied the lines of the map onto it. When he unwrapped the tube, he had a flat map.

▼ Zooming in on Earth

The detail on Earth can be shown at different sizes. As you zoom in you can see more detail. Different maps are used to study the Earth. A globe shows the whole of the Earth. A state or county map will show you a small part of the Earth, while a street map will help you find your way around a city or town.

▲ World from afar

We cannot see all the countries on a globe because some are hidden. Here you can see Oceania, and some of Antarctica and Asia.

▼ Making maps

As soon as people started exploring the world, they started drawing maps. Travellers brought back rough plans from different parts of the world. The first person to put these all together into a large map was the Greek, Ptolemy, about 1,900 years ago. But it still had many gaps – because large parts of the Earth were still unknown. Slowly, these gaps were filled in. The first complete world map did not appear until the last century.

▶ State map

Zooming in a bit more, you can see state or county details. You can also find the names and places of major cities and towns. You might use a map like this if you wanted to find out about the states of Australia. For example, from this map, can you tell in which state you would find the city of Brisbane?

The world

Here is a map of the whole world – on two pages!
It shows you all the main land areas of the world, and the oceans and seas. Can you see how much of the map is coloured blue? This is because there is so much water. Oceans, lakes, rivers and other water cover over two-thirds of the Earth's surface.

ARCTIC OCEAN

North America

NORTH ATLANTIC OCEAN

PACIFIC OCEAN

South America

North America

Population	483 million people
Climate	All types
Land features	All types
Area	24 million square kilometres

South America

Population	346 million people
Climate	Hot and wet, hot and dry
Land features	Rainforest, desert, grassland
Area	18 million square kilometres

Antarctica

Population	No permanent pop.
Climate	Always very cold
Land features	Ice and snow
Area	14 million square kilometres

Europe
Population 729 million people
Climate Mild
Land features Plains, uplands, mountains
Area 10 million square kilometres

ARCTIC
OCEAN

Asia

Europe

PACIFIC
OCEAN

Africa

Asia
Population 3,683 million people
Climate All types
Land features All types
Area 45 million square kilometres

INDIAN
OCEAN

Oceania

Oceania
Population 30 million people
Climate Hot and dry, hot and wet, mild
Land features Rainforest, desert, grassland
Area 18 million square kilometres

Antarctica

Africa
Population 784 million people
Climate Hot and wet, hot and dry
Land features Desert, rainforest, grassland
Area 30 million square kilometres

The continents

The land on the Earth's surface is split up into seven large areas that are called continents. Their names are North America, South America, Europe, Asia, Africa, Oceania and Antarctica. Some of these, such as Europe, are very crowded, while nobody at all lives permanently in Antarctica. Some are big blocks of land, while others, such as Oceania, are made up of thousands of islands — some enormous and some tiny.

If you look closely, you will see that some of the continents are joined together. North and South America are linked by a narrow strip of land, called an isthmus. Asia and Europe are really part of the same huge land mass, and only a narrow canal separates Africa from Asia.

Comparing countries in each continent

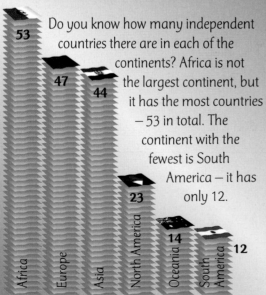

Do you know how many independent countries there are in each of the continents? Africa is not the largest continent, but it has the most countries — 53 in total. The continent with the fewest is South America — it has only 12.

Highest and lowest temperatures

North America
57 degrees Celsius
−63 degrees Celsius

South America
49 degrees Celsius
−33 degrees Celsius
14 degrees Celsius
−89 degrees Celsius

Europe
50 degrees Celsius
55 degrees Celsius

Asia
54 degrees Celsius
−68 degrees Celsius

Africa
58 degrees Celsius
−24 degrees Celsius

Oceania
53 degrees Celsius
−22 degrees Celsius

Antarctica

Europe

Asia

QUIZ

1. Which is the largest continent?
2. Which is the smallest continent?
3. Which continent has the most people?
4. Which is the coldest continent?
5. Which continent has the most countries?

Answers on page 48.

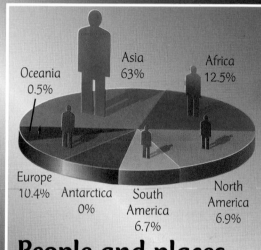

Oceania 0.5%

Asia 63%

Africa 12.5%

Europe 10.4%

Antarctica 0%

South America 6.7%

North America 6.9%

People and places

In the diagram above, the Earth is shown as a circle divided into the seven continents. It shows you how much bigger the area of Asia (purple) is than Oceania (orange). You can also see how many people live in each continent – the population. Sixty-three percent of the world's population lives in Asia while nobody lives in Antarctica.

Oceania

Antarctica

Time difference

The world spins around as it orbits, or circles, the Sun. This means that while it is daytime in one part of the world, it is the middle of the night in another! This is called time difference.

It is 7 a.m. in New York, USA, and people are getting up.

It is 12 midday in London, England – playtime!

In Tokyo, Japan, it is 9 p.m. – and time for bed.

CAPITAL CITIES OF THE WORLD

These are all the countries of the world and their capital cities.
You will see that some countries have two capital cities.

The country name is in bigger, bold type (**Antigua**), with the capital city in smaller, italic type (*St John's*).

North America

Antigua and Barbuda *St John's* ● **Bahamas** *Nassau* ● **Barbados** *Bridgetown* ● **Belize** *Belmopan*

Canada *Ottawa* ● **Costa Rica** *San Jose* ● **Cuba** *Havana* ● **Dominica** *Roseau*

Dominican Republic *Santo Domingo* ● **El Salvador** *San Salvador* ● **Grenada** *St George's*

Guatemala *Guatemala* ● **Haiti** *Port-au-Prince* ● **Honduras** *Tegucigalpa* ● **Jamaica** *Kingston*

Mexico *Mexico City*

Nicaragua *Managua*

Panama *Panama*

St Kitts Nevis *Basseterre*

St Lucia *Castries*

St Pierre and Miquelon *St Pierre*

St Vincent and the Grenadines *Kingstown*

Trinidad and Tobago *Port-of-Spain*

United States of America *Washington D.C.*

South America

Argentina *Buenos Aires* ● **Bolivia** *La Paz*

Brazil *Brasília* ● **Chile** *Santiago*

Colombia *Bogota* ● **Ecuador** *Quito*

Guyana *Georgetown* ● **Paraguay** *Asunción*

Peru *Lima* ● **Suriname** *Paramaribo*

Uruguay *Montevideo* ● **Venezuela** *Caracas*

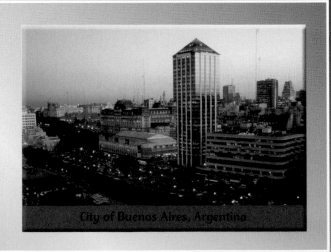

City of Buenos Aires, Argentina

Europe

Albania *Tirana*

Andorra *Andorra La Vella*

Austria *Vienna* ● **Belarus** *Minsk*

Belgium *Brussels*

Bosnia-Herzegovina *Sarajevo*

Bulgaria *Sofia* ● **Croatia** *Zagreb*

Cyprus *Nicosia* ● **Czech Republic** *Prague*

Denmark *Copenhagen* ● **Estonia** *Tallinn*

Finland *Helsinki* ● **France** *Paris* ● **Germany** *Berlin* ● **Greece** *Athens* ● **Hungary** *Budapest*

Iceland *Reykjavik* ● **Ireland** *Dublin* **Italy** *Rome* ● **Latvia** *Riga* ● **Liechtenstein** *Vaduz*

Lithuania *Vilnius* ● **Luxembourg** *Luxembourg* ● **Macedonia** *Skopje* ● **Malta** *Valletta*

Moldova *Chisinau* ● **Monaco** *Monaco* ● **Netherlands** *Amsterdam, The Hague* ● **Norway** *Oslo*

Poland *Warsaw* ● **Portugal** *Lisbon* ● **Romania** *Bucharest* ● **Russia** *Moscow*

San Marino *San Marino*

Serbia & Montenegro *Belgrade*

The Parthenon, Athens, Greece

Tower Bridge, London, United Kingdom

Slovakia *Bratislava*

Slovenia *Ljubljana* ● **Spain** *Madrid*

Sweden *Stockholm* ● **Switzerland** *Bern*

Ukraine *Kiev* ● **United Kingdom** *London*

Vatican City *Vatican City*

Asia

Afghanistan *Kabul*

Armenia *Yerevan*

Azerbaijan *Baku*

Bahrain *Manama*

Bangladesh *Dhaka*

Bhutan *Thimphu*

Brunei *Bandar Seri Begawan*

Cambodia *Phnom Penh*

China *Beijing (Peking)*

East Timor *Dili*

Georgia *Tbilisi* • India *Delhi*

Indonesia *Jakarta* • Iran *Tehran*

Iraq *Baghdad* • Israel *Jerusalem*

Japan *Tokyo* • Jordan *Amman* • Kazakhstan *Astana* • Kuwait *Kuwait*

Kyrgyzstan *Bishkek* • Laos *Vientiane* • Lebanon *Beirut*

Malaysia *Putrajaya, Kuala Lumpur*

Maldives *Male* • Mongolia *Ulaanbaatar*

Myanmar (Burma) *Yangon (Rangoon)*

Nepal *Kathmandu* • North Korea *P'yongyang*

Oman *Muscat* • Pakistan *Islamabad*

Philippines *Manila* • Qatar *Doha*

Saudi Arabia *Riyadh* • Singapore *Singapore*

South Korea *Seoul*

Sri Lanka *Colombo, Kotte*

Syria *Damascus* • Taiwan *T'aipei*

Tajikistan *Dushanbe* • Thailand *Bangkok*

Turkey *Ankara* • Turkmenistan *Ashgabat*

United Arab Emirates *Abu Dhabi*

Uzbekistan *Tashkent* • Vietnam *Hanoi*

West Bank and Gaza *Ramallah* • Yemen *Sanaa*

Africa

Algeria *Algiers* ● Angola *Luanda* ● Benin *Cotonou, Porto-Novo* ● Botswana *Gaborone*

Burkina-Faso *Ouagadougou* ● Burundi *Bujumbura* ● Cameroon *Yaoundé* ● Cape Verde *Praia*

Central African Republic *Bangui* ● Chad *N'Djamena* ● Comoros *Moroni* ● Congo *Brazzaville*

Côte D'Ivoire *Yamoussoukro*

Democratic Republic of Congo *Kinshasa*

Djibouti *Djibouti* ● Egypt *Cairo*

Equatorial Guinea *Malabo*

Eritrea *Asmara* ● Ethiopia *Addis Ababa*

Gabon *Libreville* ● Gambia *Banjul*

Ghana *Accra* ● Guinea *Conakty*

Guinea-Bissau *Bissau* ● Kenya *Nairobi*

Pyramids, Cairo, Egypt

Lesotho *Maseru* ● Liberia *Monrovia* ● Libya *Tripoli, Surt* ● Madagascar *Antananarivo*

Malawi *Lilongwe* ● Mali *Bamako* ● Mauritania *Nouakchott* ● Mauritius *Port Louis*

Morocco *Rabat* ● Mozambique *Maputo* ● Namibia *Windhoek* ● Niger *Niamey*

Nigeria *Abuja* ● Rwanda *Kigali* ● São Tomé *São Tomé* ● Senegal *Dakar* ● Seychelles *Victoria*

● Sierra Leone *Freetown* ● Somalia *Mogadishu* ● South Africa *Cape Town, Pretoria*

Sudan *Khartoum* ● Swaziland *Lobamba, Mbabane* ● Tanzania *Dodoma* ● Togo *Lomé*

Tunisia *Tunis* ● Uganda *Kampala* ● Zambia *Lusaka* ● Zimbabwe *Harare*

Oceania

Australia *Canberra* ● Federated States of
Micronesia *Palikir* ● Fiji *Suva*

Kiribati *Bairiki*

Marshall Islands *Dalap-Uliga-Darrit*

Nauru *Yangor* ● New Zealand *Wellington*

Palau *Koror* ● Papua New Guinea *Port Moresby*

Soloman Islands *Honiara* ● Tonga *Nuku'alofa*

Tuvalu *Fongafale* ● Vanuatu *Port Vila*

Western Samoa *Apia*

North America

North America contains three huge countries!
These are Canada, the United States of America and
Mexico. It also includes smaller countries in
Central America and the islands in the
Caribbean. This third biggest continent in
the world stretches from the North Pole
down to the Caribbean Sea. Here, a
spindly strip of land containing the
countries of Central America
eventually joins South America.

In North America you can see
cold white ice-caps,
mountains, rainforests,
deserts and forests – almost
all the different kinds of
land that can be seen
anywhere in the world!

▼ **An area of swampy land in the USA is
home to the very rare Everglade jaguar –
and lots of alligators too!**

Colo

◄ **Kings Canyon is the deepest
canyon in North America. Gradually
worn away by the Kings River that
flows through it, the canyon is
2,499 metres at its deepest point.**

**PACIFIC
OCEAN**

Best of North America

LARGEST GULF
The Gulf of
Mexico covers
1,543,000 square
kilometres.

LONGEST GORGE
The Grand Canyon,
a valley with
rocky sides, is 446
kilometres long.

LARGEST CRATER
Clearwater Lakes Crater
is 60 kilometres
across.

Great Bear Lake

Mackenzie River

Great Slave Lake

Hudson
Bay

ATLANTIC
OCEAN

Lake Winnipeg

Lake Superior

R O C K Y   M O U N T A I N S

Missouri River

Lake Huron

St Lawrence River

Lake Michigan

Lake Ontario

Lake Erie

Great Salt Lake

Missouri River

Mississippi River

Rio Grande

Gulf of
Mexico

▲ Many animals live in the
cold forests of Canada,
including moose and bears.
The moose is the largest deer
in the world. Its antlers can
grow up to two metres across.

Caribbean Sea

HOTTEST PLACE
In Death Valley
temperatures can
rise as high as
57 degrees Celsius.

TALLEST LIVING THING
This giant redwood
tree grows in
America. It is 112
metres high.

**LARGEST
FRESHWATER LAKE**
Lake Superior
covers 82,350
square kilometres.

A
B
D
E
F

North America People and places

Some of the richest and poorest people live here. North America contains some of the world's largest cities, but also vast areas of remote land. The USA is the richest country in the world, and big cities such as Washington D.C. are centres of wealthy living. But many people in countries like Nicaragua and El Salvador in Central America are very poor.

The USA has become wealthy because it produces most of the world's silver, nickel and copper, as well as large amounts of coal, oil and gas.

By contrast, the people of Central America are not so lucky. The country does not have many natural resources, and the wealth they create is not evenly shared amongst everybody. Most people now live in cities, while the rest are small farmers growing just enough wheat, beans and rice to survive.

The Native American Indians lived in North America for a long time before anyone else arrived. Then people from Europe came to live there, and now there is a huge number of people who have come from many different places.

② ▲ Racing monster trucks like this one is a popular sport in Canada and the USA. The huge wheels and powerful engines mean that they can easily crush ordinary cars that get in their way!

QUIZ

Can you find out which cities are in the following squares by using the grid around the map?

D10, G9, E11, F11

Answers on page 48.

① ◄ The Empire State Building is one of the most famous places in the USA. Its 102 storeys rise to a height of 381 metres.

North America Facts

Biggest country Canada – 9,970,610 square kilometres

Biggest city population Mexico City – 20,965,000 people

Most TV sets USA – 81 out of 100 people own televisions

Fewest doctors Haiti – one doctor for every 7,140 people

Fewest TV sets Haiti – 5 out of 100 people own televisions

◀ The Canadian National Tower in Canada is 553 metres tall, making it the world's tallest free-standing structure.

GREENLAND
(belongs to Denmark)

③

CANADA

②

Ottawa ■

③

①

④

Washington D.C. ■

UNITED STATES OF AMERICA

▲ Disney World in Florida in the USA is the largest theme park in the world. It covers 121,400,000 square metres, the size of 17,250 football pitches!

⑤

④

■ Nassau
BAHAMAS

MEXICO

Havana ■   CUBA

BELIZE

JAMAICA

5   2

⑤

■ Mexico City

Kingston ■

4   6

■ Belmopan

3   7

◀ The faces of four of America's presidents, carved into the side of Mount Rushmore in the USA, are the largest carved figures in the world.

l

8

1. **COSTA RICA**
San Jose
2. **DOMINICAN REPUBLIC**
Santo Domingo
3. **EL SALVADOR**
San Salvador
4. **GUATEMALA**
Guatemala

5. **HAITI**
Port-au-Prince
6. **HONDURAS**
Tegucigalpa
7. **NICARAGUA**
Managua
8. **PANAMA**
Panama

South America

South America means – jungle! The biggest tropical rainforest in the world covers an area ten times bigger than France. Through this forest winds the giant Amazon. It may be only the world's second longest river, but it carries two-thirds of the Earth's river water.

The continent contains many other marvels too. There are beautiful waterfalls, snowy mountaintops, and smoking volcanoes. It is a paradise for wildlife. A quarter of all known mammals live here, including the giant anteater and the vampire bat.

The rainforests are alive with beautiful birds, insects and animals. They also contain a staggering variety of plants, some of which give us vital medicines.

▲ The capybara is the largest rodent in the world. Rodents are animals like mice and rats, but the capybara can reach up to 1.4 metres in length!

▼ The anaconda, found in swampy river valleys in South America, is the widest snake in the world. It can measure 110 centimetres around its stomach!

Best of South America

LONGEST RIVER
The Amazon River runs for a total length of 6,448 kilometres.

HIGHEST WATERFALL
The water at Angel Falls plunges down a cliff 979 metres high.

DRIEST PLACE
The Atacama Desert has had no rain for over 400 years!

▶ The sloth is the slowest mammal on Earth. It normally moves at only 0.27 kilometres an hour – that's 15 seconds to move one metre!

Negro River

Amazon River

Purus River

Tapajos River

São Francisco

Lake Titicaca

Lake Poopo

Parana River

Uruguay River

Parana River

PACIFIC OCEAN

ATLANTIC OCEAN

ANDES

ANDES

◀ Jaguars are the largest cats in South America. They can reach up to 2.2 metres in length, and weigh up to 90 kilograms.

▶ At the junction of two rivers, 275 individual cascades form the spectacular Iguazú Falls.

LONGEST RANGE
The Andes mountain chain runs for 7,200 kilometres. It is the longest in the world.

MOST PLANTS
The tropical rainforest contains more varieties of plant than anywhere else in the world.

South America
People and places

South America is the fourth largest continent but it has one of the smallest populations. This is because much of the land is difficult to live on, and the cutting down of the rainforests has forced native people to leave their homes.

Some of South America's farms are the biggest in the world and cover areas larger than some countries. However, most are small and farmers own or rent small plots of land, struggling to grow enough food to survive.

Three-quarters of the people in South America now live in towns and cities. Many of these people are very poor and cannot afford houses. They crowd into flimsy shelters on the outskirts of towns. Meanwhile a few South Americans are very wealthy. These are mainly the landowners, factory bosses and political leaders.

Until the Spanish and Portuguese invaded in about 1500 only native tribes lived in South America. Now most people are a mix of Native American and European.

► **This Bolivian woman is dressed in traditional clothes – blankets and a bowler hat. Life in rural Bolivia has not changed for many years.**

QUIZ

1. Can you count how many countries there are in South America?
2. Can you find the capital city of the largest country in South America?

Answers on page 48.

South America Facts

Smallest country Surinam – 163,270 square kilometres
Countries where most people live in cities Uruguay – 91 out of 100 people live in cities, Argentina – 90 out of 100 live in cities
Country that produces most silver Peru – 14 percent of world total
Most TV sets Argentina – 22 out of 100 people own televisions
Fewest doctors Guyana – one doctor for every 6,220 people

◀ This beautiful statue of a bird with a snake is carved out of stone. It was made in Colombia about 2,000 years ago.

▶ Pipes like these are used by musicians who live in the Andes mountains.

■ Caracas
VENEZUELA
GUYANA
Georgetown
■ Paramaribo
FRENCH GUIANA
(belongs to France)
■ Bogota
COLOMBIA
②
SURINAME
■ Quito
ECUADOR
PERU
③
BRAZIL
③
■ Lima
①
■ Brasilia
■ La Paz
BOLIVIA
PARAGUAY
④
CHILE
■ Asunción
ARGENTINA
URUGUAY
■ Santiago
Buenos Aires
■ Montevideo
⑤

▼ Artists live in these brightly coloured flats in Buenos Aires, capital of Argentina. They have painted their houses in wonderful colours.

▼ Deforestation means cutting down forests. This is happening at an alarming rate. A total of 370,000 square kilometres was cleared between 1990 and 2000.

④

A
B
C
D
E
F
G

25

Europe

Europe is the second smallest continent in the world – less than a quarter the size of Asia. Yet it is also the most crowded, with its population contained in 47 different countries.

Europe is able to support such a large number of people because it is lucky enough to have good farmland covering half of the continent. But there is less space for wildlife. The European brown bear is one of the few big animals to live in Europe.

There is a wide variety of birdlife, as well as smaller animals such as badgers, foxes, deer, hedgehogs, squirrels and wild boar.

▲ **Copper butterflies can live almost anywhere. They are tiny, growing to only 36 millimetres across their wings.**

▲ **This fallow deer is guarding her fawn. The white spots on their coats help camouflage them amongst leaves where they live. The fawn may stay with its mother for more than a year.**

▲ **A red fox's natural habitat is woodland, but many have adapted to living in towns. They mainly hunt for food at night. They will eat almost anything, from rabbits and earthworms to fish and apples.**

Best of Europe

HOTTEST PLACE
Seville in Spain recorded a high of 50 degrees Celsius in August 1881.

LARGEST SEA
The Mediterranean Sea covers about 2,503,000 square kilometres.

LARGEST ISLAND
Britain is the largest island in Europe, covering 218,041 square kilometres.

Norwegian Sea

Barents Sea

◀ The grebe is a water bird that dives underwater to catch food such as small fish, insects, snails and shrimps. It is the only bird that can dive whilst carrying its young.

North Sea

Lake Ladoga

Lake Onega

Baltic Sea

Volga River

Rhine River

Elbe River

Vistula River

Don River

Bay of Biscay

Loire River

Seine River

Dnepr River

CARPATHIANS

Tagus River

PYRENEES

Alps

Danube River

Black Sea

◀ The European peregrine falcon is the fastest animal in the world. It can dive at speeds of over 280 kilometres per hour, that is 75 metres a second.

Mediterranean Sea

LARGEST MAMMAL
Brown bears can grow to a height of 1.2 metres.

SLOWEST BIRD
The Eurasian woodcock can only fly very slowly, travelling 2 metres a second.

A

B

C

D

E

F

G

27

Europe
People and places

Europeans have changed the world.

Despite its small size, Europe has produced writers, artists, scientists and explorers whose lives have influenced the rest of the world since the time of the ancient Greeks.

Most Europeans are descended from the tribes that roamed the area long ago. More than 70 different languages are spoken by the people living in Europe today. Over the last fifty years, many new settlers have come to Europe from Asia, Africa and the Caribbean.

Europe is a wealthy continent, with many modern kinds of industry. Today, Europe produces more manufactured goods than any other of the world's continents. Several countries, though, especially those in the east, remain poor.

▲ The London Eye is the world's highest observation wheel, standing at 136.1 metres. Views all over London can be seen from the top.

IRELAND

▲ Venice in Italy is a city built on water. Boats, such as these gondolas, are used to get around. They are moved with long poles that touch the bottom of the canals and drive the gondolas forward.

SPAIN
PORTUGAL
Madrid ■
■ Lisbon

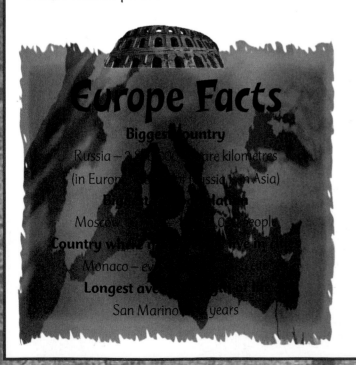

Europe Facts
Biggest country
Russia – 3,800,000 square kilometres
(in Europe – most of Russia is in Asia)
Biggest city population
Moscow – people
Country where people live longest
Monaco – every people
Longest average life
San Marino – years

◄ Neuschwanstein castle in Germany was the model for the Magic Kingdom castle in Walt Disney's theme park in the USA.

28

◀ Greece is very popular with tourists. They visit the islands to enjoy the hot sunshine and visit the beautiful old buildings.

QUIZ

Find the European countries, hidden in these jumbled up names.

OLD SCANT   ANGRY ME
MARK END   RAIN BIT
SIR USA   CAR FEN

Answers on page 48

▲ France is the most visited country in the world. The Eiffel Tower is one of its main attractions.

SWEDEN

FINLAND

NORWAY

Helsinki

Oslo ■   Stockholm ■   ■ Tallinn

RUSSIA

ESTONIA

SCOTLAND

Edinburgh ■

■ Riga

DENMARK

LATVIA

Moscow ■

ublin

Copenhagen ■

LITHUANIA

ENGLAND

Vilnius ■

WALES

6

Cardiff ■

■ Minsk

London ■

BELARUS

3

12

Berlin ■   Warsaw ■

Brussels

GERMANY

POLAND

5

■   BELGIUM

Kiev ■

8

UKRAINE

■ Paris

4

1

SLOVAKIA

FRANCE

15

Vienna ■   ■ Bratislava

MOLDOVA

■ Budapest

■ Chisinau

7

AUSTRIA

HUNGARY

2

14   3

ROMANIA

ITALY

■ Belgrade   ■ Bucharest

11

2

SERBIA &

13

MONTENEGRO

BULGARIA

I

■ Sofia

Rome ■

16

9

Tirana ■

4

ALBANIA

10

GREECE

■ Athens

1. **ANDORRA**
   Andorra La Vella
2. **BOSNIA-HERZEGOVINA**
   Sarajevo
3. **CROATIA**
   Zagreb
4. **CZECH REPUBLIC**
   Prague
5. **ICELAND**
   Reykjavik
6. Kaliningrad
   (part of Russia)
7. **LIECHTENSTEIN**
   Vaduz
8. **LUXEMBOURG**
   Luxembourg
9. **MACEDONIA**
   Skopje
10. **MALTA**
    Valletta
11. **MONACO**
    Monaco
12. **NETHERLANDS**
    Amsterdam,
    The Hague
13. **SAN MARINO**
    San Marino
14. **SLOVENIA**
    Ljubljana
15. **SWITZERLAND**
    Bern
16. **VATICAN CITY**
    Vatican City

CYPRUS   ■ Nicosia

A
B
C
D
E
F
G

Asia

Asia is big in many ways. It is the biggest continent, covering a third of the world's land area. It also has the biggest population by far – nearly two-thirds of all the people in the world live in Asia.

Asia also has the biggest range of scenery. It contains the highest place on Earth (Mount Everest) and the lowest (the Dead Sea), as well as deserts, jungles and frozen plains. There are vast stretches of empty land which is no good for farming, but there are also river valleys which have some of the best farmland anywhere in the world.

◀ The black woodpecker has the loudest tap in the world! It can be heard up to 1.8 kilometres away!

Black Sea

Mediterranean Sea

Tigris

Euphrates River

Red Sea

Arabian Peninsula

▲ The Siberian tiger is the largest big cat in the world. It is also the rarest as there are probably only a few hundred left in the wild.

Best of Asia

FRESHWATER SEALS
The Lake Baikal seals are the world's only freshwater seals.

HIGHEST MOUNTAIN
Mount Everest, on China and Nepal's borders, is 8,863 metres high.

LOWEST PLACE
The Dead Sea is situated 408 metres below sea level.

30

◄ The caracal is a desert cat. It once roamed over large areas, but is now rarely seen.

▷ Tree frogs live on the edge of Asia's rainforests. Their bright green colouring makes it difficult for hungry birds and snakes to see them.

Lena River

Ob River

Angara River

Lake Baikal

Yenisey River

Irtysh River

Gobi Desert

Caspian Sea

Aral Sea

Syr Darya River

Amu Darya River

TIEN SHAN

Huang He

HINDU KUSH

HIMALAYAS

Chiang Jiang

Indus River

Thar Desert

Ganges River

Arabian Sea

Bay of Bengal

Mekong River

South China Sea

PACIFIC OCEAN

A
B
C
D
E
F
G

LONGEST POISONOUS SNAKE
The King Cobra in India can grow to 5.7 metres in length.

31

Asia
People and places

Asia contains a huge number of different races.

Each speaks a different language and follows a different way of life. There are Mongolian herdsmen living on the vast grasslands, and city-dwellers living in modern Japan. Oil brings wealth to many Arab people, while most people in India work on small farms. Big cities such as Tokyo are among the most crowded in the world. The world's major religions – Christianity, Islam and Hinduism – all began in Asia.

▲ A few Mongolian people live on the grassland steppes of central Asia, where they raise herds of goats, cattle and yaks. They live in felt-covered tents called yurts.

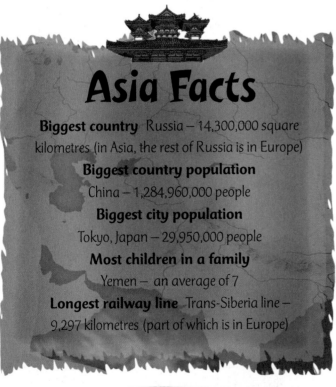

Asia Facts

Biggest country Russia – 14,300,000 square kilometres (in Asia, the rest of Russia is in Europe)

Biggest country population
China – 1,284,960,000 people

Biggest city population
Tokyo, Japan – 29,950,000 people

Most children in a family
Yemen – an average of 7

Longest railway line Trans-Siberia line – 9,297 kilometres (part of which is in Europe)

TURKEY
Ankara ■
13
19
9 10
8
11
4
16
Riyadh ■
SAUDI
ARABIA
Sana ■
YEMEN

▲ In India and other Asian countries, bicycles are used as taxis. These taxis are called rickshaws – they are also used for moving heavy goods about.

◀ Muslims believe that the Dome of the Rock in Jerusalem is the holiest place on Earth. It was built over the rock from which, according to Muslim belief, the Prophet Muhammad rose to heaven.

A
B
C
D
E
F
G

▶ China holds a New Year's Day parade. A group of people dress up in a large dragon costume. They believe that the dragon helps prevent evil spirits from spoiling the New Year.

④

QUIZ

1. Which one country would you have to travel through to get from Iran to India?
2. Mongolia shares a border with two other countries, what are they?

Answers on page 48.

1. **AFGHANISTAN** Kabul
2. **ARMENIA** Yerevan
3. **AZERBAIJAN** Baku
4. **BAHRAIN** Manama
5. **BANGLADESH** Dhaka
6. **BHUTAN** Thimphu
7. **GEORGIA** Tbilisi
8. **IRAQ** Baghdad
9. **ISRAEL** Jerusalem
10. **JORDAN** Amman
11. **KUWAIT** Kuwait
12. **KYRGYZSTAN** Bishkek
13. **LEBANON** Beirut
14. **MALDIVES** Male
15. **NORTH KOREA** P'yŏngyang
16. **QATAR** Doha
17. **SINGAPORE** Singapore
18. **SOUTH KOREA** Seoul
19. **SYRIA** Damascus
20. **TAJIKISTAN** Dushanbe
21. **TURKMENISTAN** Ashgabat
22. **UNITED ARAB EMIRATES** Abu Dhabi
23. **UZBEKISTAN** Tashkent

■ Moscow

RUSSIA

■ Astana

KAZAKHSTAN

Ulan Bator ■

③

MONGOLIA

JAPAN

Tokyo ■

15

Beijing ■

18

21   23

Tehran

12

20

IRAN

1

CHINA

⑤

④

■ Islamabad

T'aipei ■

TAIWAN

NEPAL

PAKISTAN

Kathmandu ■

6

■ Muscat

Delhi ■

OMAN

5

INDIA

②

MYANMAR (BURMA)

Hanoi ■

LAOS

Vientiane ■

Manila ■

PHILIPPINES

Rangoon (Yangon) ■

VIETNAM

Bangkok ■

THAILAND

■ Phnom Penh

CAMBODIA

Bandar Seri Begawan ■

BRUNEI

14   ■ Colombo

SRI LANKA

MALAYSIA

⑤

■ Kuala Lumpur / Putrajaya

17

◀ This army of terracotta warriors is in the world's largest tomb in China. Qin Shihuangdi's, Emperor of China, was buried here 2,210 years ago.

INDONESIA

■ Dili

EAST TIMOR

■ Jakarta

Africa

Africa is the second biggest continent in the world. You could fit Europe into it nearly three times over! But fewer people live in the whole of Africa than in Europe.

There are many wonderful natural sights in Africa, such as Mount Kilimanjaro and the wildlife of the jungles and grasslands.

The longest river, the Nile, flows through the northeast of the continent. It provides water for the farmland along its banks. But much of Africa is an extremely hot and dry place to live because it lies across the Equator. The largest desert in the world, the Sahara Desert, takes up most of the north of the continent, but there are tropical rainforests further south.

Even though there are plenty of minerals, such as gold, diamonds, and even oil, two-thirds of the world's poorest countries are on the African continent.

▶ The African elephant is the largest land animal in the world. It can grow up to 7.5 metres tall and can weigh as much as 90 adult humans!

▲ The lion is the largest big cat in Africa. It can grow to 3 metres in length.

ATLANTIC OCEAN

Best of Africa

TALLEST MAMMAL
The giraffe can grow to a height of 6 metres. Its legs are 1.8 metres long.

HIGHEST MOUNTAIN
Kilimanjaro soars to 5,894 metres.

▲ The meerkat is a type of mongoose. It lives in large groups of up to 30 animals in connecting underground burrows.

LARGEST BIRD
The ostrich grows to 2.75 metres tall and weighs up to 156 kilograms.

BIGGEST DESERT
The hot Sahara Desert covers 9,269,000 square kilometres.

Africa
People and places

Africa is a very large continent, but it has few people living there.

Nigeria has the biggest population with 108 million people, but a lot of other countries have much smaller populations – less than five million.

African people come from many racial groups. In the north, most are Arabs. South of the Sahara Desert, most people are black. They are divided up into over 800 different groups, each with its own language, religion and way of life.

Very few people live in the deserts or the dry grasslands. The most crowded areas are the Nile Valley, the Algerian coast and the South African coast.

Over 60 percent of Africans live in villages. They grow crops and raise cattle and other animals to feed themselves. This is a hard way of life, because the soil is poor and the climate is harsh.

▼ Camels are still a very important method of transport in Egypt. They are known as 'ships of the desert', and can travel for days without drinking or eating.

▲ These children from the Masai tribe live in Kenya. The traditional clothing of the Masai people is a single piece of cloth wrapped around them. These children are wearing traditional decorative beads.

▲ The Bolga people of Ghana paint their houses in bright colours. Most are farmers whose main crop is cacao beans. They sell these beans to other countries who use them to make chocolate!

Africa Facts

Biggest country Sudan – 2,505,815 square kilometres

Smallest country Seychelles – 455 square kilometres

Biggest city population Cairo, Egypt – 10,961,000 people

Shortest people Pygmies – about 140 centimetres

Largest producer of gold
South Africa – 33 percent of world total

Most children in a family
Niger – an average of 7

Shortest average length of life
Botswana – 35 years

QUIZ

Africa is the continent with the most countries.
1. Can you count how many there are?
2. What is the most easterly country in Africa?

Answers on page 48.

TUNIS
Algiers
Rabat
MOROCCO
TUNISIA
Tripoli
Surt
Cairo
ALGERIA
Laayoune
EGYPT
WESTERN SAHARA
Nouakchott
MAURITANIA
MALI
NIGER
CHAD
ERITREA
Asmara
Khartoum
DJIBOUTI
Djibouti
Niamey
Bamako
NIGERIA
Abuja
SUDAN
Addis Ababa
IVORY COAST
Yamoussoukro
LIBERIA
Monrovia
CENTRAL AFRICAN REPUBLIC
Bangui
ETHIOPIA
SOMALIA
Mogadishu
CAMEROON
Yaoundé
CONGO
Libreville
GABON
UGANDA
Kampala
KENYA
Nairobi
DEMOCRATIC REPUBLIC OF CONGO
Brazzaville
Kinshasa
TANZANIA
Dodoma
Luanda
MALAWI
ANGOLA
Lilongwe
ZAMBIA
Lusaka
MADAGASCAR
Antananarivo
Harare
NAMIBIA
ZIMBABWE
MOZAMBIQUE
Windhoek
BOTSWANA
Gaborone
Pretoria
Maputo
SOUTH AFRICA
Cape Town

1. **BENIN** Cotonou, Porto-Novo
2. **BURKINA FASO** Ouagadougou
3. **BURUNDI** Bujumbura
4. **CAPE VERDE** Praia
5. **COMOROS** Moroni
6. **EQUATORIAL GUINEA** Malabo
7. **GAMBIA** Banjul
8. **GHANA** Accra
9. **GUINEA** Conakry
10. **GUINEA BISSAU** Bissau
11. **LESOTHO** Maseru
12. **RWANDA** Kigali
13. **SÃO TOMÉ** São Tomé
14. **SENEGAL** Dakar
15. **SIERRA LEONE** Freetown
16. **SWAZILAND** Mbabane, Lobamba
17. **TOGO** Lomé

◀ Cape Town, co-capital of South Africa, was the first white settlement in South Africa. It was founded in 1652. Cape Town lies at the foot of Table Mountain.

A
B
C
D
E
F
G

37

Oceania

Oceania is really more than one continent. It is the name we give to a group of islands covering an enormous area in the Pacific Ocean. The biggest of these islands is Australia, and there are 14 other countries. Oceania is the smallest of the continents.

The next biggest parts of Oceania are New Zealand (which is made up of two islands) and Papua New Guinea. The rest of this strange continent is made up of at least 30,000 small islands.

Much of this area has been isolated from the rest of the world for millions of years, so many unique animals are found here. Animals like the duck-billed platypus, the kangaroo and the koala are found nowhere else in the world.

▲ Koalas are only found in Australia. They are covered with soft, thick brown and grey fur. They eat the leaves and young shoots of eucalyptus trees.

INDIAN OCEAN

▼ Ayers Rock, now called Uluru, in Australia is the largest free-standing rock in the world. It is 300 metres high and over 600 million years old.

▲ The duck-billed platypus is one of the strangest mammals in the world. It has fur like a mammal, but it has webbed feet like a duck. It also has a bill like a bird, and it lays eggs!

Best of Oceania

LARGEST BUTTERFLY
Queen Alexandra's birdwing has a wingspan of 280 millimetres.

LONGEST CORAL REEF
The Great Barrier Reef in Australia is 2,025 kilometres long.

OLDEST ROCKS
Zircon crystals from Australia are 4,276 billion years old.

A
B
C
D
E
F
G

▶ The beautiful mountainous island of Moorea lies in the South Pacific. The warm temperatures rarely fall below 21 degrees Celsius.

PACIFIC OCEAN

Torres Strait

Gulf of Carpentaria

Coral Sea

Timor Sea

Great Sandy Desert

Gibson Desert

Murchison River

Great Victoria Desert

Simpson Desert

Nullarbor Plain

Lake Eyre

Diamentina River

Murray River

Tasman Sea

Flinders Island

SOUTHERN OCEAN

Cook Strait

HIGHEST GEYSER
The Pohutu in New Zealand, reaches heights of 30 metres.

LONGEST LIVING REPTILE
Tuataras can live for an amazing 120 years.

LONGEST BILL
The Australian pelican's bill can grow to 47 centimetres.

Oceania
People and places

About 80 percent of Australians live in the south-east corner. Nearly all the major cities are here, including the capital, Canberra. The land is good for farming and the climate is mild and wet. Almost nobody lives in the centre of the country, known as the outback. It consists of vast deserts and grasslands.

Most Australians come from families that moved here from Europe during the 20th century. Aboriginals, the first people to live in Australia, now make up less than one percent of the total. However, it was not always like this. Aboriginals, like the other first people of Oceania, travelled from Southeast Asia 40,000 to 70,000 years ago. They sailed from island to island for thousands of years, setting up homes in many places. When the British came to Australia 200 years ago they destroyed the Aboriginals' way of life.

Farming and mining make Australia and New Zealand wealthy countries, and Papua New Guinea produces timber and copper. The smaller countries have little to sell and are much poorer. However, the tourist industry is growing fast in the Pacific and this is helping to create jobs and bring money to the islands.

QUIZ

Many places in Oceania take their name from early explorers who came from Europe. Can you find on the map on page 39 places named after: **James Cook, Abel Tasman Matthew Flinders, Luis de Torres Edward Eyre?**

Answers on page 48.

Oceania Facts

Biggest country Australia – 7,000,000 square kilometres

Smallest country Nauru – 21 square kilometres

Biggest city population Sydney, Australia – 3,502,000 people

Longest average length of life Australia – 80 years

Country that produces most diamonds Australia – 34 percent of the world total

► **The Sydney Opera House looks over the harbour in Australia. The building was finished in 1973.**

A

B

C

D

E

F

G

▶ The people of Papua New Guinea speak more languages than anywhere else in the world – about 869! Each language is only spoken by an average of 4,000 people.

②

PAPUA NEW GUINEA

Port Moresby ■

SOLOMON ISLANDS ■ Honiara

VANUATU

Port Vila ■

NEW CALEDONIA
(belongs to France)

③

▲ These men are sheep shearing – shaving the sheeps' coats for their wool. New Zealand has about 58 million sheep and 8 million cattle – that's about 25 farm animals to every person!

AUSTRALIA

■ Canberra

①

Tasmania

NEW ZEALAND

③ ■ Wellington

41

Antarctica

Antarctica is the most difficult place to live in the world. It is the coldest continent, and 98 percent of the land area is covered with ice and snow. Some of the ice is nearly five kilometres deep – more than ten times the height of the world's tallest building! The ice reaches out into the sea forming huge ice shelves that occasionally break off to form vast floating icebergs.

Almost nothing grows here, so it is not surprising that Antarctica has the smallest population in the world. However, a few explorers and tourists visit, and there are several camps where scientists work studying animals and the ice.

Even animals find it difficult to live here. The few that do, live mainly in the air or in the sea. Penguins, seals and whales survive because of their thick layer of blubber, or fat, which keeps them warm. They feed off fish and tiny animals called krill that live in the sea.

▲ The first person to reach the South Pole was Norwegian Roald Amundsen in 1911. This museum is dedicated to him and the British explorer, Captain Scott, the man he beat to the pole.

▲ The albatross has the largest wingspan of any living bird. Its wings measure 3.6 metres across!

Best of Antarctica

COLDEST PLACE
Vostok Station, on July 21, 1983, recorded –89.2 degrees Celsius.

DEEPEST ICE
Ice has been found to a depth of 4,776 metres.

A

B

C

D

E

F

G

The Weddell seal from Antarctica is one of the largest seals in the world, growing up to 2.9 metres long. It makes deeper and longer dives than any other seal. It has been recorded underwater for 73 minutes diving to a depth of 600 metres.

QUIZ

Which of these animals live in the Antarctic?
Polar bear
Emperor penguin
Arctic tern
weddell seal
Albatross

Answers on page

SOUTH PACIFIC OCEAN

SOUTH ATLANTIC OCEAN

Weddell Sea

Ronne Ice Shelf

■ Halley Station (UK)

Ross Ice Shelf

o South Pole

■ McMurdo Air Station (USA)

Molodezhnaya ■ Station (Russia)

West Antarctica

Dumont D'Urville Station (France) ■

Vostok Station (Russia)

■ Casey Base (Australia)

INDIAN OCEAN

The emperor penguin is the largest of all penguins, reaching a height of 1.2 metres. It raises its young on the Antarctic ice, enduring severe cold and winds.

INDEX

The numbers in **bold** type refer to main entries in your book

QUIZ ANSWERS

Page 13

1. Asia
2. Oceania
3. Asia
4. Antarctica
5. Africa

Page 20

D10 Ottawa
G9 Mexico City
E11 Washington D.C.
F11 Nassau

Page 24

1. 12
2. Brasilia (capital of Brazil)

Page 29

Scotland (OLD SCANT)
Denmark (MARK END)
Russia (SIR USA)
Germany (ANGRY ME)
Britain (RAIN BIT)
France (CAR FEN)

Page 33

1. Pakistan
2. Russia and China

Page 37

1. 53
2. Somalia

Page 40

Cook Straight G12
Tasman Sea E11
Flinders Island F10
Torres Strait C10
Lake Eyre E9

Page 43

Emperor penguin
Weddell seal
Albatross